THE ESSENCE OF
TAO

THE ESSENCE OF

TAO

An Anthology of Quotations

Compiled by *Maggie Pinkney*

THE FIVE MILE PRESS

The Five Mile Press

The Five Mile Press Pty Ltd
70 Gold Street
San Francisco, CA 91433
USA
Website: www.fivemile.com.au
Email: publishing@fivemile.com.au

First published 2006
Compiled by Maggie Pinkney
Designed by Zoë Murphy
Printed in China
ISBN 1 74178 196 5

CONTENTS

INTRODUCTION

With its emphasis on compassion and living in harmony with nature, Tao is particularly attractive and relevant to us today.

The ancient Chinese wisdom of Tao is based on the *Tao Te Ching* – a book whose origins are shrouded in mystery. Many scholars believe it was written by Lao Tzu about 600 years before Christ. According to legend, he was the keeper of the Imperial Library at the ancient capital of Loyang. Weary of government corruption, he decided to leave the city forever. On his way out, the guard of the city gates, who had heard of Lao Tzu's great wisdom, asked him to write down his teachings. This he did, over the following days, before disappearing into the desert.

The *Tao Te Ching* is the philosophical masterwork he left behind. Tao, which can loosely be translated as 'The Way' or 'The Path' is a complex and mystical philosophy, full of subtlety and paradox. And yet its sagacity and benevolence shine through. Tao, among many other things, is about using patience and understanding to work in harmony with life's circumstances.

The aim of this anthology is to make Tao more accessible to the reader with no special knowledge of the philosophy. Many of the quotations in these pages are drawn directly from the *Tao Te Ching*. Other are included because they enrich our understanding of one of the East's most profound and enduring systems of thought.

Maggie Pinkney, 2006

What is Tao?

Something infinite,

Older than heaven and earth,

Silent, solitary, and vast;

Eternal, unchanging,

Yet ever evolving

Throughout ten thousand things.

Not knowing its name,

I call it Tao.

LAO TZU

To embrace all things

means that one rids oneself

of any concept of separation:

male and female,

self and other,

life and death.

Division is contrary

to the nature of Tao.

———————

LAO TZU

The Tao is an empty vessel.

It is used but never exhausted.

It is the fathomless source

of all things upon Earth.

LAO TZU

Those who follow the Tao

are strong in body, clear of mind,

and sharp of sight and hearing.

They do not fill their minds with anxieties

and are flexible in adjusting

to external conditions.

CHUANG TZU

The Tao moves
by returning in endless cycles.
By yielding, it overcomes,
creating the ten thousand things,
being from nonbeing.

LAO TZU

Tao is more than

just a philosophy of life.

It's a whole way of life,

and the only way to realize

practical benefits from Tao

is to cultivate and practice it.

DANIEL REID

I hold three treasures

close to my heart.

The first is love;

The next, simplicity;

The third, overcoming ego.

LAO TZU

Those who have attained the Way

can respond to the unexpected

without fear,

and can escape from trouble

when they encounter it.

———————

WEN TZU

Follow the Tao,

Cultivate its ways,

And find yourself at peace.

Cultivated in your soul,

The Tao brings peace to your life.

Cultivated in your home,

It brings peace to those you live with.

Spreading it to friends and neighbors,

It brings peace to your community.

Spreading through communities,

It brings peace to your nation.

Spreading through the nations,

The Tao brings peace throughout the world.

How do I know this?

Because it begins with you and me.

———————

LAO TZU

The follower of the Way

conserves his energy

by according with,

and adapting to,

each new situation.

HUA CHING NI

Find Your True Self

Be still

And discover your center of peace.

Throughout nature

Everything in the universe moves along,

But each returns to its source.

Returning to center is peace.

Find Tao by returning to source.

LAO TZU

My soul can lead me to healing.

I will become one with my true self.

———

DEEPAK CHOPRA

When you try to understand everything,

you will not understand anything.

The best way is to understand yourself,

and then you will understand everything.

SHUNRU SUZUKI

Everything has its own place and function.

That applies to people,

although many don't seem to realize it,

stuck as they are in the wrong job,

the wrong marriage, or the wrong house.

When you know and respect

your Inner Nature,

you know where you belong.

———————

BENJAMIN HOFF

This above all – to thine own self be true,

And it must follow as night the day,

Thou canst not then be false to any man.

WILLIAM SHAKESPEARE

Resolve to be thyself and know that he

Who finds himself loses his misery.

MATTHEW ARNOLD

Your goal is to find out who you are.

A Course in Miracles

One should treat oneself

as one does one's friends –

critically but with affection.

FRANCES PARTRIDGE

Reason is your light

and your beacon of Truth.

Reason is the source of Life.

God has given you Knowledge,

so that by its light you may

not only worship Him,

but also see yourself

in your weakness and strength.

KAHLIL GIBRAN

Have patience with all things,

but chiefly have patience with yourself.

Do not lose courage

in considering your own imperfections,

but instantly set about remedying them –

every day, begin the task anew.

ST FRANCIS DE SALES

A wise man sees his own faults.

A courageous one corrects them.

Your vision will become clear

only when you can look into your heart.

Who looks outside dreams.

Who looks inside, awakes.

CARL JUNG

There is no need to run outside

For better seeing.

Nor to peer from a window. Rather abide

At the center of your being:

For the more you leave it, the less you learn.

———————————

LAO TZU

The more faithfully you listen

to the voice within you,

the better you will hear

what is sounding outside.

DAG HAMMARSKJÖLD

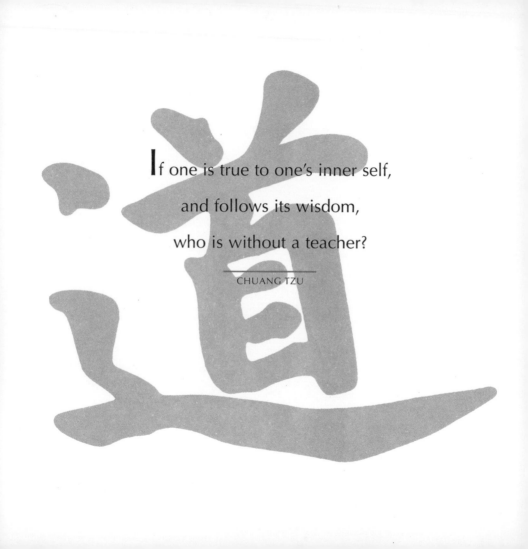

If one is true to one's inner self,

and follows its wisdom,

who is without a teacher?

CHUANG TZU

Truth is within ourselves; it takes no rise

From outward things, what'er you may believe.

There is an inmost center in us all,

Where truth abides in fullness.

ROBERT BROWNING

If you look to others for fulfilment,

you will never be truly fulfilled.

LAO TZU

At One with Nature

The best people are like water.

They benefit all things,

And do not compete with them.

They settle in low places,

One with Nature, one with Tao.

———————

LAO TZU

The world is my body.

The mountains are my bones;

the forests are my skin;

the rivers are my blood;

the air is my breath; the sun is my sight.

In my love for the earth,

I balance all life.

DEEPAK CHOPRA

Forget not that the earth
delights to feel your bare feet,
and the wind longs to
play with your hair.

KAHLIL GIBRAN

The human system is a microcosm

of nature and the cosmos;

health and longevity can only be cultivated

by harmonizing the human system

with the rhythms of Heaven and Earth.

—————

DANIEL REID

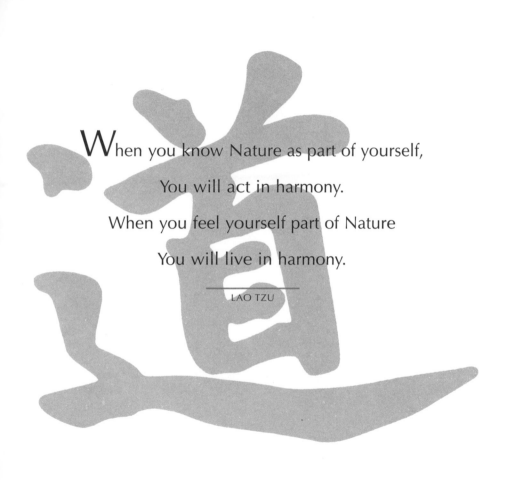

When you know Nature as part of yourself,

You will act in harmony.

When you feel yourself part of Nature

You will live in harmony.

LAO TZU

Shall I not have intelligence
with the earth:
Am I not part leaves and
vegetable and mold myself?

HENRY DAVID THOREAU

Climb the mountains,

and get their good tidings.

Nature's peace will flow into you

as the sunshine into the trees.

The winds will blow their freshness into you,

and the storms their energy,

while cares will drop off like autumn leaves.

—————————

JOHN MUIR

He who is in harmony with himself

is in harmony with the universe.

MARCUS AURELIUS

All things are connected.

Whatever befalls the earth

befalls the children of the earth.

CHIEF SEATTLE

Live each season as it passes;

breathe the air,

drink the drink,

taste the fruit …

HENRY DAVID THOREAU

Do you imagine the universe is agitated?

Go into the desert at night,

and look out at the stars.

This practice should answer the question.

LAO TZU

Keep your mouth closed.

Guard your sense.

Temper your sharpness.

Simplify your problems.

Mask your brightness.

Be at one with the dust of the earth.

This is primal union.

LAO TZU

We have to take the whole universe
as the expression of the one Self.
Only then does our love flow to all beings
and creatures in the world equally.

SWAMI RAMDAS

We too should make ourselves empty,

that the great soul of the universe

may fill us with its breath.

LAURENCE BINYON

The universe is a single life
comprising one substance
and one soul.

MARCUS AURELIUS

Every part of nature teaches

that the passing away of one life

is the making room for another.

HENRY DAVID THOREAU

The universe is sacred

You cannot improve it.

If you try to change it, you will ruin it.

If you try to hold it, you will lose it.

———————

LAO TZU

The world is not to be put in order;

the world is order, incarnate.

It is for us to harmonize with this order.

HENRY MILLER

United be your purpose,

harmonious be your feelings,

collected be your mind,

in the same way as all the various aspects

of the universe co-exist in togetherness,

wholeness.

RIK SAMHITA

Now I see the secret

of the making of the best persons.

It is to grow in the open air,

and to eat and sleep with the earth.

WALT WHITMAN

Balance and Harmony

Happiness is not a matter of intensity,

but of balance and order

and rhythm and harmony.

THOMAS MERTON

The single most important point
to remember about polarity
is that *yin* and *yang* energies
are not separate energies;
they are one and the same energy,
but with two different charges.

MANTAK CHIA

There are as many nights as days,

and the one is just as long as the other

in the year's course.

Even a happy life cannot be

without a measure of darkness,

and the word 'happy' would lose its meaning

if it were not balanced by sadness.

It is far better to take things as they come along

with patience and equanimity.

CARL JUNG

Know the masculine,

but keep to the feminine.

———————————

LAO TZU

My shadow self and I

have the same goal –

to join the light.

DEEPAK CHOPRA

The *yin–yang* view of the world

is serenely cyclic.

———————

ALAN WATTS

Life is the blended harmony

of *yin* and *yang*.

CHUANG TZU

Under heaven

everyone knows that the existence of beauty

Depends on the existence of ugliness.

Everyone knows the capacity for kindness

Depends on the existence of the unkind.

Existence and nothingness are mutually born,

Difficult and easy complete each other.

LAO TZU

The Tao is the One.

From the One come *yin* and *yang*;

From these two, creative energy;

From creative energy, the ten thousand things,

The forms of all creation.

All life embodies *yin*,

And embraces *yang*,

Through their union,

Achieving harmony.

If only there were evil people

somewhere insidiously committing evil deeds,

and it were necessary to separate them

from the rest of us and destroy them.

But the line dividing good and evil

cuts through the heart of every human being.

And who is willing to destroy

a piece of his own heart?

ALEXANDER SOLZHENITSYN

I have learned silence from the talkative;

tolerance from the intolerant,

and kindness from the unkind;

yet, strange,

I am ungrateful to those teachers.

KAHLIL GIBRAN

Being and becoming

are the *yin* and *yang* of our lives –

one inner, one outer.

Today, we value becoming

to the exclusion of being:

we applaud human becomings.

The secret is balance.

UNKNOWN

What is born will die,

What has been gathered will be dispersed,

What has been accumulated will be exhausted,

What has been built up will collapse,

And what has been built high

will be brought low.

BUDDHIST WISDOM

Changes of every kind –

from the transitory changes of state

to deep-rooted fundamental transformation –

are brought about by the active principle, *yang*,

but it is the constructive principle, *yin*,

that causes everything to assume a stable,

concrete form or cease to exist altogether.

MANFRED PORKERT

Nothing under heaven
is more soft and yielding than water.
Yet for attacking the solid and strong,
nothing is better.
It has no equal.

LAO TZU

Compassion is, by nature,

peaceful and gentle,

but it is also very powerful.

DALAI LAMA

The opposites have a vital need for each other,

just as no human being can live fully

without relationships.

An attempt to do so

is either to stagnate or to

court mental and spiritual malaise.

———————

J. C. COOPER

We could never learn

to be brave and patient

if there were only joy in the world.

HELEN KELLER

The Tao of
Friendship

True happiness consists

not in the multitude of friends

but in the worth and choice.

BEN JONSON

When I walk with two companions

both would be my teachers:

I would choose their good traits

and follow them,

and would try to correct in myself

the faults I see in them.

CONFUCIUS

It is said there are three levels of friendship.

The first is the level of casual acquaintance.

The second is where there is sharing.

The third, considered the deepest,

is the level where we trust friends

to criticize us.

DENG MING DAO

We are all travelers

in the wilderness of this world,

and the best we can find in our travels

is an honest friend.

ROBERT LOUIS STEVENSON

A friend who truly knows you

is always with you.

CHINESE PROVERB

I want someone to laugh with me,

someone to be grave with me,

someone to please me and help

my discrimination with his or her remark,

and at times, no doubt, to admire

my acuteness and discrimination.

ROBERT BURNS

Friendship

is always a sweet responsibility,

never an opportunity.

KAHLIL GIBRAN

A friend is someone

with whom I can be sincere.

Before him I may think aloud.

RALPH WALDO EMERSON

Three types of friendship are beneficial:

they are friendship with the honest,

the sincere and the well-informed.

Three types of friendship are damaging:

they are friendship with flatterers, with hypocrites

and with the argumentative.

CONFUCIUS

The best mirror is an old friend.

It is one of the severest tests
of friendship to tell your friend his faults.
To so love a man that you cannot bear
to see a stain upon him, and to speak
painful truth through loving words,
that is friendship.

HENRY WARD BEECHER

Your friend is the man

who knows all about you,

and still likes you.

ELBERT HUBBARD

Adopt Nature's Pace

Slow down and enjoy life.

It's not just the scenery you miss

by going too fast –

you also miss the sense

of where you are going and why.

———————

EDDIE CANTOR

A good traveler has no fixed plan,

and is not intent on arriving.

LAO TZU

Do not struggle.

Go with the flow of things,

and you will find yourself

at one with the mysterious unity

of the universe.

CHUANG TZU

Our patience will achieve
more than our force.

———————

EDMUND BURKE

Never go to excess
but let moderation be your guide.

CICERO

For everything there is a season,

And a time for every matter

under heaven.

ECCLESIASTES 3: 1–8

By letting go, it all gets done.

The world is won by those who let go!

LAO TZU

The things that are really for thee,

gravitate to thee.

———————

RALPH WALDO EMERSON

Happiness is a butterfly which, when pursued,

is always beyond our grasp,

but which, if you sit down quietly,

may alight upon you.

NATHANIEL HAWTHORNE

If I keep a green bough in my heart,

the singing bird will come.

CHINESE PROVERB

Standing on tiptoe, one is unsteady.

Taking long steps, one quickly tires.

Showing off, one shows lack of enlightenment.

Displaying self-righteousness, one reveals vanity.

Praising the self, one earns no respect.

Exaggerating achievements, one cannot long endure

LAO TZU

We all go wrong

by too strenuous a resolution

to go all right.

NATHANIEL HAWTHORNE

'Ah, Miss Harriet,

it would do us no harm to remember

oftener than we do,

that vices are sometimes only virtues

carried to excess!'

CHARLES DICKENS
Dombey and Son

In action,

it is timeliness

that matters.

LAO TZU

Adopt the pace of nature:

her secret is patience.

RALPH WALDO EMERSON

After a heavy snowfall the rigid branches

of the pine break under the weight of the snow,

but the supple willow branches bend,

thus allowing the snow to slip to the ground.

TAO WISDOM

How poor are they who have not patience!

What wound did ever heal but by degrees?

WILLIAM SHAKESPEARE

Man is born soft and supple,

but in death he is stiff and hard.

Living plants are tender and pliant;

dead, they are brittle and dry.

Thus, whoever is rigid and inflexible

is a disciple of death.

The hard and rigid will be broken.

The soft and supple will prevail.

LAO TZU

*S*eize the opportunity

when it arises.

FENG MENGLONG

Learn to have the patience of a gardener.

He cultivates the soil,

plants the seeds and waters them.

Then he waits for the first shoots.

They will appear when they are ready.

CHINESE WISDOM

Never cut a tree down in the wintertime.
Never make your most important decisions
when you are in your worst moods.
Wait. Be patient. The spring will come.

ROBERT SCHULLER

Do not be desirous
of having things done quickly.
Do not look to small advantages.
Desire to have things done quickly
prevents their being done thoroughly.
Looking to small advantages prevents
great affairs being accomplished.

CONFUCIUS

Everything comes gradually,

and at its appointed hour.

———————

OVID

A Quiet Mind

Do not lose your inward peace

for anything in the world,

even if your whole world seems upset.

ST FRANCIS DE SALES

Quiet minds

cannot be perplexed or frightened

but go on in fortune or misfortune

at their own private pace

like a clock ticking in a thunderstorm.

ROBERT LOUIS STEVENSON

Great tranquility of heart

is his who cares

neither for praise nor blame.

THOMAS A KEMPIS

Silence is a great help to the seeker after truth.

In the attitude of silence,

the soul finds the path in a clearer light,

and what is elusive and deceptive

resolves itself into crystal clearness.

Our life is a long and arduous quest after truth,

and the soul requires inward restfulness

to attain its full height.

MAHATMA GANDHI

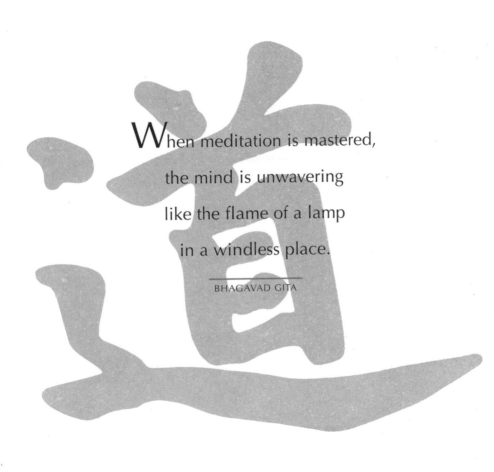

When meditation is mastered,
the mind is unwavering
like the flame of a lamp
in a windless place.

BHAGAVAD GITA

When all is done and said,

in the end you shall find,

He most of all doth bathe in bliss

that hath a quiet mind.

THOMAS, LORD VAUX

Like water,

we are truest to

our nature in repose.

CYRIL CONNOLLY

There is no need to go to India

or anywhere else to find peace.

You will find that deep place of silence

right in your room, your garden

or even your bathtub.

ELISABETH KÜBLER-ROSS

Sweet are the thoughts

that savor of content;

The quiet mind is richer than a crown.

ROBERT GREENE

Contentment

that derives from knowing

when to be content

is eternal contentment.

LAO TZU

He is richest

who is content with least,

for content is the wealth of Nature.

SOCRATES

I am indeed rich,

since my income

is superior to my expense,

and my expense

is equal to my wishes.

EDWARD GIBBON

Annual income twenty pounds,

annual expenditure nineteen pounds six,

result happiness.

CHARLES DICKENS
David Copperfield

A person who is not disturbed
by the incessant flow of desires
can alone achieve peace,
and not the man who strives
to satisfy such desires.

BHAGAVAD GITA

To live content with small means;

to seek elegance rather than luxury;

and refinement

rather than fashion…

to bear all cheerfully, do all bravely,

await occasions, hurry never.

In a word to let the spiritual and unconscious

grow up through the common.

This is to be my symphony.

WILLIAM ELLERY CHANNING

No sin can exceed

Incitement to envy;

No calamity is worse

Than to be discontented.

LAO TZU

Everything has its wonders,

even darkness and silence,

and I learn, whatever state I'm in,

therein to be content.

—————————

HELEN KELLER

Perfect happiness

is the absence of

striving for happiness.

———————————

CHUANG TZU

Fame or integrity – which is more important?

Money or happiness – which is more valuable?

If your happiness depends on money,

you will never be happy with yourself.

Be content with what you have;

rejoice in the way things are.

When you realize there is nothing lacking,

the whole world belongs to you.

———————

LAO TZU

Embrace simplicity,

Reduce selfishness,

Have few desires.

LAO TZU

True contentment

is a thing as active as agriculture.

It is the power of getting out of any situation

all that there is in it.

It is arduous and it is rare.

G.K. CHESTERTON

Drink tea

and forget the world's noises.

CHINESE SAYING

If only we'd stop trying to be happy,

we could have a pretty good time.

EDITH WHARTON

The Tao of Success

Our grand business in life

is not to see what lies dimly at a distance,

but to do what clearly lies at hand.

THOMAS CARLYLE

A journey of a thousand miles
must begin with a single step.

LAO TZU

People often fail on the verge of success.

By giving as much care to the end

as the beginning,

There will be few failures.

LAO TZU

When you get into a tight place

and everything goes against you,

till it seems as though

you could not hang on a minute longer,

never give up then,

for that is just the place and time

that the tide will turn.

HARRIET BEECHER STOWE

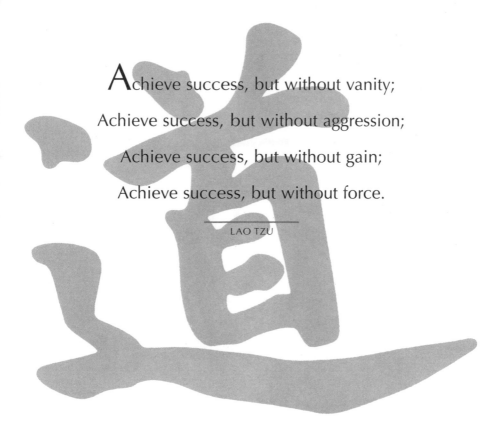

Achieve success, but without vanity;

Achieve success, but without aggression;

Achieve success, but without gain;

Achieve success, but without force.

LAO TZU

If you achieve success you will get applause,

and if you get applause you will hear it.

My advice to you concerning applause is this:

enjoy it but never quite believe it.

—————————

ROBERT MONTGOMERY

You are more likely to succeed
if you know your strengths and weaknesses,
your place in society
and your worth.

FENG MEGLONG

Angels fly

because they take themselves so lightly.

G. K. CHESTERTON

No truly great man
ever thought himself so.

WILLIAM HAZLITT

Deal with the difficult,

While it is still easy.

Solve large problems

When they are still small.

Preventing large problems

By taking small steps

Is easier than solving them.

Therefore, the Tao follower

Anticipates and lives wisely,

By small actions

Accomplishing great things.

———————

TAO WISDOM

There is nothing of which every man is so afraid

as getting to know

how enormously much he is capable

of doing and becoming.

SÖREN KIERKEGAARD

Knowing others is intelligence;

knowing yourself is true wisdom.

Mastering others is strength;

mastering yourself is true power.

If you realize that you are truly rich.

LAO TZU

Tao Wisdom

Kindness in words creates confidence.

Kindness in thinking creates profundity.

Kindness in giving creates love.

———————

LAO TZU

The whole idea of compassion
is based on a keen awareness of the
interdependence of all these living beings,
which are all part of one another,
and all involved in one another.

THOMAS MERTON

I do not value those

who broadcast others' failings,

subordinates who slander their superiors,

those who are brave but lack manners,

those who are decisive but lack consideration.

CONFUCIUS

I will nurture every need but one –

the need to judge others.

DEEPAK CHOPRA

I do not bully the weak,

nor do I fear the strong.

ZUO QUINING

Do not conquer the world with force,

For force only causes resistance.

Thorns spring up when an army passes.

Years of misery follow a great victory.

Do only what needs to be done,

Without using violence.

LAO TZU

The superior man

loves his soul.

The inferior man

loves his possessions.

CONFUCIUS

The more a man lays stress
on false possessions,
and the less sensitivity he has
for what is essential,
the less satisfying his life is.

CARL JUNG

It is necessary to be noble,

and yet take humility as a basis.

It is necessary to be exalted

and yet take modesty as a foundation.

LAO TZU

To judge a man,

compare his words with his deeds.

LIU XIANG

When the Great Tao is lost,

we have 'goodness' and 'righteousness'.

When 'wisdom' and 'sagacity' arise

we have hypocrites.

LAO TZU

The person of superior integrity
does not insist upon his integrity.
For this reason, he has integrity.
The person of inferior integrity
never loses sight of his integrity.
For this reason, he lacks integrity.

———————

LAO TZU

To lead people, walk beside them.

People do not notice the existence

of the best leaders.

The next best are honored and praised.

The next, are feared.

And the worst are hated.

When the best leader's work is done,

people think they've done it themselves.

———————

LAO TZU

The sage does not accumulate.

The more that he expends for others,

The more does he possess of his own;

The more that he gives to others,

The more does he have himself.

———————

LAO TZU

Force is followed by loss of strength.

This is not the way of Tao.

LAO TZU

If one desires to receive

one must first give.

This is called

profound understanding.

LAO TZU

There is no greater disaster

Than enemy-making,

For then you lose your treasure,

Your peace.

When conflict arises,

Compassion always prevails.

———————

LAO TZU

In dwelling, live close to the ground.

In thinking, keep to the simple.

In conflict, be fair and generous.

In governing, don't try to control.

In work, do what you enjoy.

In family life, be completely present.

LAO TZU